Birthdays
Before and After

By

Puma Perl

BEYOND BAROQUE BOOKS

Birthdays Before and After

Editor
Iris Berry

Introduction
Kat Georges

Cover
Chelle Mayer

Beyond Baroque Literary Arts Center

Beyond Baroque Books
681 Venice Boulevard
Venice, CA. 90291

310-822-3006
www.beyondbaroque.org

About Beyond Baroque Books

Beyond Baroque Literary / Arts Center is one of the nation's most successful and influential grassroots incubators of the literary arts. Founded in 1968, and housed in the original Venice City Hall building in Venice, California, Beyond Baroque is a nonprofit public space dedicated to cultivating new writing and expanding the public's knowledge of poetry, fiction, literature, music, and art through cultural events and community interaction. In 1971, Beyond Baroque began issuing chapbooks in order to publish works by both emerging and established poets. Titles include the first book from Los Angeles's inaugural poet laureate, Eloise Klein Healy, and works by Dennis Cooper, Amy Gerstler, Bill Mohr, Harry Northup, Holly Prado, and Wanda Coleman, amongst others. The Center's current press, Beyond Baroque Books was launched in 1998. It has published works by Jean-Luc Godard, Jack Hirschman, Diane di Prima, David Meltzer and others. The Pacific Coast Poetry Series imprint was launched in 2013 and has published three titles, including the anthology *Wide Awake: Poets of Los Angeles and Beyond*. Beyond Baroque Books continues to unearth cult rarities, as well as collections by noted performance poets, educators and cultural leaders.

Introduction

Back in 2008, I was fortunate to read Puma Perl's powerful chapbook *Belinda and Her Friends*, a short collection filled with poems I described as "chiseled in granite with fingernails." Since then, with the additional chapbook "Ruby True" and two full-length collections, *knuckle tattoos* and *Retrograde*, Perl's work has led her to become a major force in the international underground poetry scene, with packed readings in Los Angeles, San Francisco, Prague, London, as well as her native New York City.

The energy Perl generates in her work is addictive. Perl's poems often involve characters with names ringing clear like those names that splash through a Lou Reed or Leonard Cohen song. Scenes are painted that bring to life the streets of the East Village and Lower East Side—streets filled with people—the hopeful and the hopeless, the lovers and the loveless, the monied and the poor—people expanding a landscape dreamt up by the author, with tags of reality between clouds of imagination.

Through the years, Perl's work has retained the familiar ring of her subject matter, while growing in style and form. This latest collection, *Birthdays Before and After*, is exquisite as an example of a poet truly taking the reins of her art and merging the present, past, and haunting future in word paintings searing in their intensity.

The thirty-two poems in *Birthdays...* address birthdays of the poet and others as touchstones: annual celebrations of survival and hope. Perl starts in search of a perfect day, driven by a survey of friends and relations to decide for herself in the book's opener, "The Most Perfect Day." By the book's close, she's shattered the need for ideals, and discovers solace in "The Most Perfect Imperfect Day" with its stunning closing lines,

> *all I have left is you and*
> *what could have been on those most perfect*
> *imperfect days.*

Throughout *Birthdays...* Perl's narrative elements of place and pathos become symbols for the poet to explore more deeply than ever, leading to such exemplary poetic revelations as, from the poem "Birthdays Before and After":

Nobody is lost
Just a little bit broken.

This collection shows Perl shedding emotion and superlatives as she faces the death of heroes like David Bowie and Lou Reed, and personal losses that grow more frequent with age. With each loss and gain, words and worth become more focused, as Perl muses in "What I Need and Don't Need,"

You are not the same as me
the same as him the same as her
Yet
Wait until we leave
Outsides no longer
hide who we are
Wait until we're nothing
but the inside.

Through this reverberating collection, Perl offers poems that are funny, hard, fearless, and sad—a kind of Burroughs-esque cut-up, taken, of both a singular life, and a community of friends, a new definition of family, that is as universal as it is unique.

Kat Georges
Poet, Playwright, Publisher

*Dedicated to the musicians
painting pictures*

TABLE OF CONTENTS

"Now I got these diaries that have the greatest hero a writer needs, this crazy fucking New York."

- Jim Carroll, *The Basketball Diaries*

The Most Perfect Day

What was the best day of your life?

Louie says it was the day
I took him to a double feature on Forty Deuce.
Indiana Jones and The Warriors.

My mother used to say it was the day
she had a baby. Me. Unfortunately,
it went rapidly downhill from there.

Juliet told me it was the first time
she saw JayZ, a day filled with boys,
friends, hip-hop, and alcohol.

Annie would choose a day
of pick-up trucks, shotguns,
and stone drunk love.

The first time I met Lee McGrevin
was one of those days.

It was during the Beast Crawl.
Toxic Abatement.
Razor threw a barbecue.
My rock and roll LA friend tried to talk me out of going.

Go hang out in the Haight, he advised.
Go to Amoeba Records.
Go to Golden Gate Park.
Why do you want to hang out
with a bunch of poets? He demanded.
Separate yourself.
You're a star. You're from New York.

He finally stopped talking.
Then he wanted to have phone sex.

His ignorant snobbery had eliminated all chances.

Iris called me at my crack house motel
on San Pablo. The Berkeley Inn.

You're coming, she said. *I'll get you.*
My West Coast sister
whom I'd never seen in person.

Jason called. A writer friend
going back to the old MySpace days.
We'd never met in person, either.

Wait for me. I'll pick you up.

An hour later, Jason and his Colorado skater buddy
pulled up to the crack house parking lot, backed
the rental car into a telephone pole, and we were off.

We were off.

A backyard filled with punks and poets,
flowers, a barbecue pit, overflowing trays
of food, back steps leading into the house.
Iris and I sat on those steps and took a picture,
Razor bought a book. He insisted.
Support the traveling poets, he said.

I'd found my tribe.

Someone knocked at the gate.
I opened it. Bucky Sinister.
Punks and Elephants,
a favorite poem of mine.

I walked into the kitchen
to get a cool drink of water.
The most beautiful man
I'd ever seen stood at the sink,
washing dishes.
Lee McGrevin.
I've seen many beautiful men before

and since, but none so unexpectedly,
and none of them were washing dishes.

Later, we all walked down to the deck
of a nearby restaurant and shared the best
poetry reading in the immediate universe.

The best and the most beautiful.

The temperature dropped and we ended the evening
around the bonfire telling old stories, sharing wounds.
Lee fanned the flames. I photographed his knuckle
tattoos. *LOST SOUL*. Somehow, we got on to the subject
of the Tompkins Square Park cannibal, who allegedly
chopped his girlfriend up and fed her to the homeless.
The motive seemed to be the same as your average developer.

She had a rent-controlled apartment on 9th Street,
and she was sick of him hanging around.

Razor expressed some doubts about the veracity of the story.
He lived in the park back then, ran the kitchen,
and he swore those stews were vegetarian.

The next day, Bill Gainer read a poem about our evening.
All I remember is the line,
And then they started talking about eating people!

The morning after Lee died I went to the gym.
I braced myself against the bars and did more leg-ups
than ever before.
It's always the things you don't brace yourself for,
I thought, staring at nothing as I rose and fell, rose and fell.
Rose and fell.

The Needle and the Damage Done came up on IPOD shuffle.
Should have been *A Perfect Day*.
I guess the angels had their hands full

3

and were too busy to program my music that morning. Still, should have been *A Perfect Day.*

Could have been the best day of my life.

Birthdays Before and After

On the day before my birthday,
I reschedule a doctor's visit, rearrange a maintenance
appointment, withdraw money from the bank in case the tip jar is
undernourished, return a FedEx package, pick up posters,
and buy a couple of pumpernickel bagels

The Kossar's guy winks at me and gives me four
I tell myself I'll freeze two
I tell myself little lies all the time

I had wanted to wear my new Saint Anthony medal,
a gift from a friend, but the clasp is broken
At least it's not lost
Broken, not lost
Like me

Scott Wannberg used to write me
birthday poems every year, addressed
to The Queen of New York City
David Smith called me that too, in memory
of those Chelsea Hotel stays
We'd cruise around in my old Maxima,
Scott riding shotgun,
stream of consciousness ramble
mixed with song lyrics,
David laughing in the back

Maybe tomorrow, on my birthday,
David will mix one of those retro drinks he loves
A sidecar or an Old Fashioned
Or perhaps they might not remember
When you're newly dead you have a lot more
on your mind than a Lower East Side birthday
Perhaps next year they will message me
Or I might make it to the bar myself,
body left behind in somebody's dirt,

ask David for a Dirty Martini extra dry
or a Margarita in case we wind up
in a warmer climate
Salt on the rim

After I finish the errands
I go to the library,
sit at the corner computer
and write, print, edit, print
Poems about relationships more layered
and complex than the people in them
Words last longer but don't taste as sweet
The best things in my life never happen
We make choices, all of them loaded,
write more than we talk and barely touch
Hold off for fear of fucking up what is
already fucked and it will pass,
tension turning to tedium
Cross the line, risk decimation,
we've been there before
No interplanetary wars
or national chaos results
from our blind stupidity

Freedom in the emptiness of not mattering

I can't hurt more than I did
and the loves of my life can't die twice

I toast myself at midnight
A beer, a shot, half a peanut butter cookie
The dog and I ate the bagels

On the morning of my birthday I do laundry
Lose socks
Forget to eat
Go to the library
Sit at the corner computer
Freedom, again, in nothing
Crashed computers, stolen cars, missing wallets

bring negative space, like a Texas sky

All of it, missing, not lost
Or lost, but not yet completely broken

Tonight, we come together,
raise a glass to birthdays and music
and memories and poetry and everything
lost, and everything found

Maybe Jimmy the Saint will find his way
to David's bar and finally meet up with Scott
They'll get along fine and nobody will worry
about aging fathers in Oregon
or oxygen tanks or heart surgery
or baseball bats or dental work
or lost machetes in Bushwick
They'll do some poems and play some music

Like we always do.

Nobody is lost.
Just a little bit broken.

On the Morning of My Birthday

On the morning of my birthday,
I bought a box of strawberries from the man
   who stands on the corner of Grand and Clinton
They were moldy
I ate mashed potatoes for breakfast

On that same morning, somebody smashed the headlights
                  on my car

It's an omen, I told a friend who called
                  with celebratory wishes
Mostly, I didn't pick up the phone

You're just having a bad birthday, she assured me
How do you tell them apart? I wondered

It was still morning
I walked the dog in circles
Smiling, she tackled me in the yard

Earlier that day, there had been an earthquake in Chile
Tsunami waves reached Japan
In New York City, the temperature hit 88 degrees,
             well above the norm
All across the country, Republicans prepared to flood the
network
In the midst of the turmoil, Mickey Rourke turned 63

September 16
Mexican Independence Day
Somewhere, there were parades and fireworks

On the Lower East Side, children headed back to school
       following a two-day holiday
The next day, an Amber Alert would go out for the little girl
       who lives on the fourth floor of my building

I threw out the moldy strawberries, and fell asleep, dreaming
                    of the car, enclosed in silver gray shroud
I once knew a man who wrote new poems for every reading
Then he threw them away
I wish he were here tonight
Like his poems, he was beyond description and danced
                                    like an angel

I woke up in time for Happy Hour, mojitos, Margaritas
Met my friends for a while, bought rice and beans
                                from a supermarket
Don't know if they were good, but at least the mold,
                        if any, was undetectable.

Eclipsed

The moon, you say, as explanation
I don't ask for more
Eclipsed

I wait in the East Broadway subway breeze,
consider the intentions of a moonless night
The consequences

A girl in metal tattoo armor passes,
proud of her shoulders
Painted people acknowledge each other,
like drifters and bikers

Not this girl, in her long pink tank top
and tribal forearms
She gets off at Second Avenue

You know exactly how to be, you say
As if I had a choice
Eclipsed

I return to the moon, its moods
Its questions

Art.
A family member or boarder,
devoid of origin?

Can we pack our drives away,
and wander with empty suitcases?

Will we merge poetry and sound and cum and blood?

Can we fuck out of bounds, without safe words,
against tenement walls?

The 6 train is slow as baseball
At 14th, I push my way out, onto the 5

I exit at 86th, lost,
as I sometimes am,
waking at 4AM,
half asleep,
too confused to
find the bedroom
door

I center myself
Proceed southeast,
toward light and music
and Margaritas

Sick and tired of knowing
how to be

Eclipsed, again.

Collaborators

Caramel syrup
Swells my lip

I sit on a bus stop bench
eating only the vanilla
ice cream

Less soothing
than it sounds

One of many
tastes that fall short
of expectations

Five dollars
and I threw half
of it in the garbage

I'd had another
five in my pocket
but I gave it
to the homeless girl

She was sitting on a
cardboard sign, arguing
with her boyfriend

He pretended
to be passed out

Maybe he was
She said it was her birthday

Maybe it wasn't
Or was

I gave her the five,
birthday or not

We're Virgos,
struck by Mercury

Or pretending
to be

She hugged me
and cried,
hard

Beautiful girl,
she looked like Kim,
my designer friend
Nose ring and all

I don't know
if you're supposed to
feel good when you do
these things

It's like shooting dope
Lasts a minute
and you're back
where you were

Sitting on cardboard

An hour later
I'm tossing out
vanilla ice cream
and thinking
about the things
I shouldn't do
and probably will

Wondering

How do we compensate
for the mistakes
we're about to make

There is little doubt
that we'll fuck up

My lip is swollen
and cut

This morning,
I found
some balm
in my pocket

Easier to heal
the present
than the past

Even ice cream
has a price.

The Beauty of Nothing

In dreams and New York City
You can pretend
there are no hurricanes

Buildings erupt,
tower over us
No sun fights through
Shadows hit concrete

But still we pretend
there are no tornadoes

In dreams and New York City
Silence engulfs the platform
after the subway pulls out

No silence greater
than a missed connection,
an empty station

Yet I keep pretending
that my life is full and noisy
I just can't hear it

In dreams and New York City
Vacancy is an art unto itself
The beauty of nothing prevails.

Black Leopards

The second time we got together
you noticed that
I wore a different bra

Black instead of leopard
Or the other way around

Yes, I change regularly, I noted
That's good, you observed

Everything was good
Except for the circumstances

Four years went by, or three, or five
Never thought time would move that fast
Or that hours could feel so slow

This morning the mirror shocked me
Distracted, I put sunblock in my hair
Wiped the excess onto my skin
Greasy hair is preferable
to the light hitting my face

None of us have any
Vitamin D left
in our systems,
decimated by decades
of shades and black clothes

You and I have black hair
We wear hats
Sit under trees or in dark bars
Liked each other a little too much
Until we had to go

Last month we met by chance
Drank whiskey in a booth
near the window

Lost soul mates, you called us
In other words, hopeless

Time keeps flying by
We never catch up to it,
always a few years behind
or barely ahead

I still wear black and leopard
Reminds me of everyone
Lost souls, missing bodies
Knuckle tattoos

And there is us
Left behind
like broken umbrellas,
wet and forgotten
in the trunks of cars.

The Stand

On the day after the election
I forgot how to say "Good Morning"
Wandered
in early darkness
Nobody spoke

One year later
I can't say "Happy Birthday," either
How do you wish someone
a wonderful year or a great day?
Sometimes I send birthday greetings
and write "despite it all"

Despite the Stephen King story
in which we live, despite
The Twilight Zone climate change
Despite the blaring television news
Despite the birthdays rolling on

Destruction
runs through my blood
Obliterating spirits
deep as the land
It is no longer
an option
to look away

There are short distractions
Red velvet cake,
Alejandro's songs,
Ninth innings

Like baseball, every day
is a new game with the same
broken rules and broken bats
Upon awakening,
I no longer want to die
I want to kill

I've noticed
that more people want to fuck me
than they did last year
I'm the same, a year older,
no better, not much worse
Doesn't seem to matter
when it comes to desire

The writer from 11th Street
seeks a DeBeauvoir
for his angst-ridden Sartre soul
The poet I threw out
no longer hates me
The married friend resurfaces
as a dark-haired Spencer Tracey,
I'm his Katherine Hepburn
in a rock and roll t-shirt
The comic, the ex-junkie,
the astronaut, the entertainer
All wrapped up
in a Ray Charles song

Everyone reaching,
reaching for something
to fill the void of our today

Usually, I'd rather
walk the dog
But occasionally fall
for the wrong man
at the wrong time
in the right moment
Because it's all we have

One moment that feels
a little bit right
or at least
not completely wrong.

The Last Collage

When I go out walking
I don't look back at the moon
It feels like those last days
when I belonged to you
But now I'm only repeating
what we already know
There was never any chance
Just style and suicide notes
and two chords, less than jazz
The way you liked it
Most of the weekend is spent
sober and hibernating
except for the walk
down Canal Street,
looking for Keith Haring,
finding only violins and cellos
Sorry for being nice
If you want to clean my windows
I'll give you more than I had
Sorry for being stressed
It's the journey and the frequency
Whichever way you want it
The last band is on and I watch
Like it's the Easter Parade
Distant, somewhere on the avenue
I try to call and your mailbox is full
Sorry I keep postponing
Sorry I keep saying "sorry"
when, really, all I want is out.

Reading Bukowski "On Love," New Year's Eve, 2018

Two pasteles
Five shots of coquito
Three Twilight Zone episodes
An ongoing flirtation
Email trails
Poems
An unexpected plan
Rice and beans
A drunken phone call
A supermoon
An ex-boyfriend's message
Motown in the hallway
Game of Thrones
A small cup of ice cream
A broken mug
Redemption song
The Honeymooners
The family next door
An almond croissant
A cold walk
A dog
Heat
Four shots of coquito
A window
A bed
On Love
A coulda and a shoulda
One shot of coquito
A bed
On Love
Happy.

The Night That Bowie Died: A Dream

Glitter, silver and blue and gold
rained down upon the tiles
I wandered through the streets
Into the home of a stranger
Musicians and artists filled the front
room
Everyone mourning David Bowie
Beautiful dark eyes and skin that glowed
I was the only pale white person there
A record spun on the turntable
Don Cherry, singing *Autumn Leaves*
First time I'd ever heard Don Cherry sing
We moved to the music
A woman handed me an intricately
embroidered pillow, electric pinks
and greens
She said it would keep me safe
Suddenly, a man entered the house
I saw him! He shouted
I'm going after him!
Everybody jumped into shoes and coats,
ran out the door
Cars sped off
Standing alone, I waved the pillow
in the air
Its owner was driving away
This guy stole his saxophone reeds,
she yelled out the window
We've gotta get them back!
I stumbled across a bridge
in my torn brown slippers,
doubled over in grief, talking to myself
A little boy asked me if I was all right
I entered a large hotel,
rode the elevator to my room
It was filled with people,
talking and smoking

Nobody saw me
Glitter, blue and silver and gold,
rained down upon us

I left the room and found a bar
Two people I knew sat at a small round table
They laughed at the glitter in my hair

In Bowie's honor, I ordered a mint julep
I don't know why
It just seemed right

I toasted the light
and the darkness,
and the glitter
rainbow
before us,
silver and blue and gold
raining down
upon us all.

March Monday Minutia

4:09 AM
I wake
Life on Mars
on repeat
in my head
Sound loop
Won't stop
I pick up a book
Look at the phone
Read messages
Doesn't stop
Monday has crept in,
trailing remnants
of minutia
Cable problems
A badly written book
The wrong prescription
Bisque instead of buff
A malfunctioning sensor
The fabric of my life
with shows and trips
in between
I give up
Brew vampire coffee
while the sun rises
menacingly
and the river colors
turn.

Vampire Coffee

Yesterday, I made the coffee three times.
First, I forgot the water.
Next, I forgot to change the grounds.
Third time, I got it right.
The percolator was sick of me by then.
It emitted a high-pitched groan,
like the vampires
in the book I'm reading.
As they turn,
the heart grows a brain,
thoughts invade their minds,
they try to shake them off,
the sun burns into their skin.
No longer human,
they're blood-sucking creatures,
undead, immortal.
Once in a while,
they fall in love.

Sublime Flavors

A quarter century
of sobriety
did not change
my belief
that dispensations
should be given
for sipping beer
on hot stoops,
the way we did
when cops were too busy
busting drug markets
to care much
about public drinking

Another two anniversaries
passed
I traded 27 years
for a shot of Jameson
By that time, the jungle
had changed into a zoo
Gates protected stoops,
festooned with warnings
against sitting or loitering
You couldn't even smoke
a damn cigarette
without passersby
waving their arms
and coughing

My building
is a high rise
21 floors
We have no stoops
On summer evenings
the men play dominos
and the women
gossip on the benches

Sometimes there's beer
Paper bags and straws
after sunset

The first time
I drank beer again
was not on a stoop
Not even Coney Island
or Yankee Stadium

It was a winter morning
on the Lower East Side
He'd left half a can
of Budweiser's
on the coffee table
Flat, warm beer
Gray skies
Yet still intoxicating
Tasting like memory
of all the sticky nights
that came before.

Anniversary, Unframed

I woke up at 7AM with a burning need to know the date
of my only legal union. The others are unstamped.
There might have been an informal marriage, begun
on October 24th. My one wedding, such as it was,
took place in that same month. Seems to be a popular time
for ceremonies. The anti-April. A safe distance from June.

On three hours sleep, I pulled myself up, too focused
on the task to look for my eyeglasses, and rustled through
the file cabinet for copies of my documents, in the process
knocking down some framed pictures. Jimi at Monterey,
Bob Dylan at Hammerstein Ballroom. Shattered, naked, broken,
shards of glass surrounding my bare feet. I swept up, squinting,
stepping gingerly, fighting an urge to plunge jagged crystals
into my stomach or neck, wondering how do people do it,
wondering how people don't do it, wondering if other people
stare into the tracks as they stand on the edge of subway
platforms, or am I the only one so mesmerized by the rails?

I'm no longer sure what is universal thought, or normal
behavior, I've strayed too far and cannot or will not commit
to forever or even to a little while, am unable to take vows
of sobriety or maintain the friendships required to preserve
them, forget to call my elderly aunt and uncle on holidays,
twice I have thrown the percolator basket lid in the garbage,
which makes me hate myself, hate myself more than I did
thirty years ago, staring into the mirror outside Schachter's
Baby Supplies on Avenue A transfixed by my own dishevelment.
That's three decades past and allegedly I've redeemed
and atoned, but somehow, I skipped the learning how to live part.
People who know what to do would never stand in the living
room half blind and barefoot sweeping up glass, they know
when they got married and whether they divorced, they are not
stumped and confused by the questions on passport applications.

How do you do things? How do you know? Are there secrets
hidden in the hearts of the majority, reasons to get up in

the morning, innate abilities to hang window shades and tie
shoes, love you forever or more than a year, know what to do,
remember your wedding date and your marital status, know how
to do it, stop after one, stop after six, stop after twelve,
know when to stop, when to laugh, what's not funny,
I don't know, do they say *I don't know?* When do you cry?
When do you stop? What do you know? How did you learn?

I threw the jagged pieces in a heavy garbage bag, added
tiny glass crystals and crumbs, an empty can of Progresso
chicken soup with wild rice, tied it up, placed it in the blue
container downstairs. I'm pretty sure I removed the label
and washed the tin can. I know about garbage. I know
about parking spots, library hours, street signs, road maps,
subways, and cars. I'm most interested in things that move.

October 28th. My wedding date.
The day after Lou Reed's death. Janis Joplin died October
4th, John Lennon was born October 9th, the same birthday
as his second son, Sean. Dates carved into memory.

October 28th. My wedding date. Our wedding date.
We got married on that day, or so the license proclaims.
We took a car service to Brooklyn.
I don't remember how we got back to 10th Street
or what we really thought of the whole event. I think
I got drunk. It felt like I was going to the dentist.

I don't know if we ever got divorced. I don't think
so, even though allegedly you remarried. You're not
here to tell the story. I wonder if you remembered
our anniversary. I wonder about your last thoughts,
sitting in your car, the gun shaking in your hand.

It was in the early hours of February 21st.
A wintry day.

If you'd only waited until October 28th,
maybe you'd have seen another Spring.

Daylight Savings Time

First thing
in the too late morning,
I dropped
my favorite coffee cup,
swept up black chips
and slivers,
wondering
why everything feels
so hard,
simple things
like boiling eggs,
breathing

A casual friend
(meaning we never
much liked each other)
told me once
about her mother
who moved to Arizona
and did just one thing a day

Today, she'd say,
*I'm going to the bank
Tomorrow,
I'll do the shopping*
We agreed that her life
seemed sad and terrible
Now, I understand
You need something
in front of you
to get out
of the house
An escape hatch,
a simple goal

In New York,
one thing sometimes

leads to other things
Possibility is always a possibility
In Arizona,
her mother drives alone
in her car
She parks
in the strip mall
Returns her library book
Picks up her dry cleaning
Maybe
that's all she's got
Some days,
buying soup,
walking the dog,
are all I've got
If I stand perfectly still
in the sun,
grounded
in motorcycle boots,
there may be more

Some days,
walking to the store
is harder than
boiling eggs
I heat up soup
and binge watch
America's Next Top Model
An autistic girl
forgets her lines
A former stripper
is sent home
They go to China
I eat my soup
Finish the next episode
Walk the dog
Some days
it's what I've got.

Without Snow

Are you lonely?
I don't understand
the question
Or why you asked
I don't even know the answer
If I did, I'd never admit it
Not to you

It's like asking tropical islanders
if they like snow
Maybe they are missing something,
without snow
But how could they know?

I don't speak
the "we" language
I eat
all the chicken legs
and sleep
diagonally
across the bed

When I was a kid,
my father ate
the chicken legs
I cried
and my mother yelled at him
He left the table and closed
the bedroom door
Fell asleep
on top of the blankets
Stayed on his side
of the bed

I started eating my meals alone
It doesn't matter
if I eat a baked potato
Or a steak

Or not at all

You withdraw the question
There is no good answer
"Yes" implies need
"No" implies rejection
I say nothing
Silence is an art
Or a weapon

It's Easter Sunday
Last night,
I forgot to look
for the last blue moon

There are ten eggs,
one apple, one orange,
and a Dixie cup size
ice cream container
in my refrigerator
Caramel cone
The refrigerator
looks lonely
I live without snow.

Gutter Angels

We meet out by the airport
in a low-rent hotel in Queens
It's easy to get lost
on dark streets
that lead nowhere
except to low-rent hotels
out by the airport
So anonymous
you'll never find them again

As always, you're ambivalent,
not sure if you really want
me or him or maybe some girl
out in New Jersey
Even low-rent hotels
cost more than we're worth

Inevitably
we move to cars,
parking alongside fire hydrants,
across from city playgrounds,
hiding impotently
beneath trees
Watching you unzip
is the best part

We don't believe in afterward
A laugh
Share the last drops
of whiskey
from the half pint bottle
beneath the seat
Drop me on the corner
Hope the security guard's
asleep

There are no angels here
on Water Street
Just a few seraphim,
invisible to most,
lying quietly
in the gutter.

Discretion

Nobody is safe from a writer.
I am not even safe from myself.

In a few years, after it has ended badly,
as we know it will, I'll write about you.
Only you will know. I'll change your name
and your height, your age, your vocation,
but you will know, you will remember
the rooftop and my lost bracelets, the story
of the rehab towels, the homeless lady
on the Bronx bench who mistook you
for her husband. You will learn about
my intentions to thoroughly clean
and scrub my apartment before your first visit;
I never got beyond throwing out the bath
mat and buying a new soap dish. You'll
relive the night we fucked in the ally
and all those corner tables and car rides,
your hands my mouth, only we know.
I will remember the little things, like the way
you never said my name for fear of calling
out the wrong one when you returned home
to your predominant life, the glue, the fabric,
and my care in preventing endearments
to fall from my tongue just in case those words
were somebody's property. As you were.
I will write about waiting for you to arrive, time
slipping by with so little to waste, expiration
dates glowing like the candles I never lit
since we met only in daylight. Nobody saw you
standing on South Street but me, we wore
cloaks of invisibility, caught only by the gods.
I looked into the magic glass and saw my heart.
I carry memories like knives, cut deeper, bleed
less, publish another book, plug in my cables,
take the car to the shop, it's rattling and so
is yours but not like mine, not the cable
or the car or the glint of marbles caught

in the curb sparkling in the Brooklyn sun
where we sit on benches watching helicopters
circling like vultures, eating calzones, drinking
iced coffee, until our time is up. The bell rings,
and I write another poem, wish I had a drink.
I am not allowed to miss you I can only want you.
I look at photographs of another man who loved me.
He's smiling on a Lower East Side September day
and I try to figure out why I never saw the depth
of that smile in his short life, probably because
I was the one who wiped it from his eyes. I promised
to live until I die, I promised not to leave one second
before the door opens for the last time, I'll light
the books on fire, throw the words to the air.
nobody gets hurt, nobody knows. Only you.

A Couple of Shots

A couple of shots later
We wind up onstage singing a Stones song
A couple more and we're leaning against the wall
I ask how are you, and we talk of blood moons,
full eclipses, and loss, why lately it always comes
back to loss, buildings falling, streets caving,
dying alone while we bang our heads uselessly,
pockets too small to carry everybody's keys.

It only takes a shot to remember and five or six
to forget, we stop at four, a number good enough
but not great, and we are all on stage like Judy
or Lenny or Billie, trying on the truth if only for
a minute, a couple of shots later and we are backed
against the wall again, singing a Ramones song while
the full moon thinks about waning but decides to
hang around, just for another couple of shots.

Memorial Day Morning

I woke up dreaming

We sat in a window booth
Drinking whiskey
Looking out on the dark street
Night turned to afternoon
A table in an Italian place on Court Street
Or maybe the hole in the wall Mexican joint
Fish tacos and Margaritas

Always random and deserted
Wears off like heroin and I'm left
Listening to Lucinda
Another holiday morning
More dark coffee
One-part longing, one-part regret

The night before, it may have rained
I walked, no hat, no umbrella,
no romance, just the smell
of wet dog and muddy pavement

There is no Lucinda
without heartbreak
The taste of bourbon and cigars
lingers like memory

Today is a New York holiday
The transplants are gone
Streets are deserted and promise nothing
Neither do we
Unlike the streets, we are not empty
Two parts longing, one-part regret.

Shooting Normal

So many pictures
of normal
Arks
Lives
Houses
It's 3:37 AM
Everything is broken
Too late to get Diva
Every time you leave
I walk with her
Now she's asleep
in her dog bed
surrounded by toys

Shots of tequila
lined up
on the bar
I love
the formation
Daylight
A good time
to forget
the moment
and talk
of regret,
last chances
No boats
no decks
no Christmas parties
no mothers
no fathers
nobody's arms
in the air
in my photos
No normal
Just broken

We sit
on barstools
and remember
how it felt
when the subway
door closed,
your kid
left behind,
standing alone
on the platform
Arks and houses
Normal
For those
who matter

I'm still the girl
you wanted
to fuck
on the football
field
In my school,
we had no fields,
no proms
no clubs
just cigarettes
on the back
of the bus,
and Coney Island
street corners

Normal people
sit on couches,
eat at tables,
kids drink milk
I sipped my
morning coffee,
ate my cheese
Danish, walked
down the block
to third grade

purgatory
It's 3:55 AM
Too late
to get the dog
She's sleeping
Everyone is sleeping
Everything is broken
Water bursts
through walls
Pictures fall
Broken dreams
of missed
connections
airports, fences,
floods, bicycle
wheels, stuck
in the mud

It's too early
to get the dog.

What Kind of Woman?

What kind of woman could resist
a man who tastes like a Margarita?
Possibly, most women
I wish I were most women

My life. I don't how I got here
Windows and doors remain unlocked
It no longer matters. I want to stay and I want to go
Always. We linger outside bars and clubs
Everybody says good night and nobody leaves

I wore an Indian print dress to my wedding,
a fake ring to rent an apartment
Tenth and B, over the DMZ
Purple walls in the bedroom,
bathtub in the kitchen,
windows watching buildings
turn to dope spots

The baby tossed in his crib
The bus rattled the dishes
The doorbell didn't work
The floor leaned to the east
I nailed a cabinet to the wall,
put up fake sea blue tiles above the sink,
and magic jungle wallpaper for the baby
We had an air conditioner that didn't work,
a rocking chair, an old gold couch
The streets called.

What kind of woman doesn't want
a loyal, hardworking husband?
The baby never slept at night
The husband always phoned during
our afternoon nap
He set the alarm each weekday morning
to WCBS and smoked two cigarettes
and went to work

On Sundays, he wore his blue terry cloth robe
watched "Kojak," showered, shaved, went to bed early,
so he'd be rested enough to work another week

He had routines
What kind of woman doesn't want
a baby's father with routines?
We were the only couple in the park
All of the other mothers
had welfare cases and missing fathers
What kind of woman wants a welfare case?
What kind of woman smashes her jewelry in a rage?
What kind of woman writes poems
and burns them in the kitchen sink?
What kind of woman stops nursing a baby
so she can shoot dope?
What kind of woman?

What kind of woman can't resist the taste of a Margarita,
loves men with OCD, a touch of bipolarity?
What kind of woman?

The kind of woman who fucks in cars
and sleeps alone, the kind of woman men
always want and never keep,
the kind of woman who always
leaves first, the kind of woman whose sex partners
aren't her boyfriends and whose boyfriends
aren't her sex partners
A very important kind of woman
who doesn't matter to anyone
A woman who knows where the moment is
but loses the years, a woman with a bad
decision, a left turn that never went right.

A woman who can't resist the taste of a Margarita
Who writes the script before the story starts
Who wears secrets like lockets around her bare neck
Who hides in parks and libraries and subway cars
What kind of woman are you? she's asked
A woman
with a taste
for a Margarita.

The Taste of Rebellion

What did your rebellion taste like?
Mine tasted like long-haired boys
Sounded like 4AM rock and roll,
felt like the bottom
of my mother's staircase
after she kicked me out
for coming home too late

My rebellion tasted of not going back,
smelled like $34 in my wallet,
dug into me like the knife
resting in a sheath on my hip
the day I changed my name
to Puma, just like my knife

My rebellion felt like never going home,
Feelings began in my legs,
exploded like the orgasms
I'd never even had yet,
smelled like pot and silk scarves
burning shade on lightbulbs,
looked like paisley,
reds and blues melting
on purple
Sounded like Jimi and Janis
before they reached 27
and draped the Fillmore in black

Nobody witnessed my rebellion,
everybody caught up in their own
My family had already labelled me
crazy, hopeless, a lost cause,
a loser nobody would love
They were wrong and they were right

His rebellion was dropping out
of Bronx Science, hiding a gun
in his bureau, black jeans so tight
he "customized" them
with slits up the calf
and could hardly walk up the five flights
leading to our railroad apartment
with the police lock, the brick wall,
the loft bed, the bathtub in the kitchen
Where we lived in our shared rebellion

Our rebellion was his criminality,
my welfare, our books and music,
the dog he called Stagger Lee,
nights in Tompkins Square Park
days on St. Mark's Place,
armed love, cigarettes
leather jackets

My surrender was to heroin,
His was to money
A baby born in the middle
of the surrender
His rebellion would be raves,
speed, cars, girls, and survival

The drugs are gone
Stagger Lee was stolen
from outside a bodega
and his owner's life surrendered
to the gun held in his own hand

My rebellion is quiet and solitary
Broken down Tuesdays
and hot summer days when life
seems to go on too long

Today is Wednesday, July 4th
Fireworks but no celebration
I order Chinese food and search
for a black and white movie
If new Coltrane tracks can be found
Maybe there's still some hope
for rebellion without surrender.

(Thank you, Marty McConnell for the poetry prompts)

Used Car Love
(with thoughts of Anthony Bourdain)

You say you had a lot of love
I say I had a lot of cars
and cheap hotel rooms
You had a few hotel rooms
but yours were classier,
overlooking parks and mountains
Your love had views
My love had brick walls,
Bukowski vibes,
and stained towels

The cars were cleaner
I've always had a preference
for two door models
Their sleek exterior
and sneaky leg room

Lives lived
on different planets
Family dinner conversations
in hieroglyphics
Love is a foreign country
Excavations
Ridge walking
Landing on Delancey

In the end
I catch you
alone
You seem smaller
and a little scared
Unprepared

For me,
it doesn't matter
I've got a foothold
on the other side,

waiting on the corner
in the dope dealer's boots
Buildings looming
Even your vision
is distorted
We live in shadows

You say you had a lot of love
I say I had a lot of cars
Don't pity me
I always
liked to drive.

It's Not Depression, It's August

City thunderstorms
take a brief respite as
the sun sets on Charlie Parker
and the park stills while
the Sturgeon Moon rises,
last full moon of summer
Strings of 90-degree days
have gone into hiding
I'm considering a day at the beach
when the heat returns,
pressing in like jailhouse grilled cheese
I walk downtown streets and wear black
The temperature shoots up toward 100
September's cooler but brings another birthday
and I've already had so many
Why do I need more?
Why do I need more of anything?
I have enough pairs of boots and black jeans
If only the black wouldn't fade
If only I wouldn't fade
and stay the same or better,
or even in a holding pattern
of mind and body and acceptance.
I won't be rich or famous
I won't be beautiful, or loved,
I won't even be dead.
Why do we need August anyway?
it's like a bad play that never ends
No Exit scored by the Eagles
Nothing good happens in August
My hair sticks to my forehead
I look goofy in pictures
and decide to give up smiling
Which won't be difficult
Maybe give up talking, too
And opinions
And thoughts
Nobody wants thoughts

Somebody told me who I wasn't yesterday
Someone else told me who I was
A third explained what a corporation is
A fourth defined "gentrification"
Why bother to talk at all?
People's intelligence rises
as temperatures fall
Look for me in February
I'll be wearing boots and black jeans
Just like August but smarter.

What I Need and Don't Need

My clothes
Stuffed into garbage bags
For 3 weeks I lived out of a carry-on bag
More than I brought on a 2-month bike trip

That is all I need

I unpack the black plastic
red ribbon-tied bags
Every shirt or scarf or sweater
I unfold
would look better on somebody else

I promise myself
to give my leopard scarves to Sam
My heart-shaped collection to Rick
My band shirts to Ange
My tight skirts to the skinny girls
My silk dress to Jane
My workout gear to anyone
more virtuous than me

I have 40 unmatched earrings
100 single socks
I even have unpaired shoes
due to my tendency of walking
harder on one side than the other

I'm fucked only from the neck up
Although I'm clearly
Anatomically
A woman

What a cosmic joke that was
I don't need your undying love
or devotion
Just a road map and a flashlight

27 more times around the solar system

Don't get nervous
People tend to worry when
you wanna give your shit away
Like I'm really gonna kill myself
Because I lost some stuff

I can't kill myself
That's established
It's been done
and 4AM phone calls and railroad
stations will haunt me forever

I lose stuff all the time
But when you lose the only 2 things
you really need
you stop giving much of a fuck
about the rest

Like people
Once you've lost
the one you loved
they're all about the same

Flesh and blood and bone
Covered up by words and stature
Fat or thin
Botox wars
Young beauty

And without it
you get to be invisible
See everything
Hear it all
without filter
Nobody's watching

I know how to do that

Every good criminal does

But I'm not that kind of criminal any longer
Just a bill paying American thief
with 17 more pocketbooks
and 9 more wallets
than I need

Life is so simple
without the trimmings

And don't get me wrong
I'm not Eckhart Tolle
blissing out on a park bench

Homeless is only fun if you've never been
Homeless
Spiritual quests, suburban ennui,
adventure

Not the same as a bottle of Wild Irish
and a doorway
Not the same as a kid
who's been thrown away,
who had no choice but to run

Life can be simple
without everything we thought we'd die without

Like "I'd die if I didn't write"
No, it will take a lot more than that to kill me
Can't write? Think
No computer? Pen
No bed? Floor
No dope? Sick

None of it kills you

My friend,
Bob Hart,

was killed by a very long life
He wrote new poems for each set
in his small exquisite print
and threw them away
Ephemeral moments

He had a tomato garden in Queens
loved his hobo life, his trains,
and a well showered woman

I can't read my writing
So I type
in the library
every day
and remember
how I loved his life, too

Last time we danced he was 81
and still loved what he had
which means he had it all
A tomato, a bunch of postcards,
and handfuls of crumpled poems

Most poets are just too serious
There are a billion poems out there to read
Does yours make any difference?

I've lost all my poetry
3 times
An evil lower east side genius
told me
"Write some more"
The only true words he ever spoke
There is no antidote to evil
But those 3 good words were scattered
with the rest of his ashes on 3rd Street

Giving up is so much harder than giving in
and the result is the same
We leave through the same door

Just a little bit larger

I know the words to every song about nothing
Oh Sweet Nuthin, Ain't Got Nothing
You got nothing, you got nothing to lose
and Nothing Compares to You

Nothing is free
Like nobody is free
until everyone is free

Remember that one?

Long dark streets await

Empty is not the same as hollow

You are not the same as me
the same as him the same as her

Yet

Wait until we leave

Outsides no longer
hide who we are

Wait until we're nothing
but the inside

Zoe Says/I Break

(For Zoe Hansen)

Zoe stands
at the mic
in her Rainbow glory
Raff's red dress
Leopard stilettos
Roxy Hotel
Dirty Martinis
Cold French fries

She always looks
like a million dollars
even when
she costs forty-nine cents

I was born broken
Zoe says

We were all born broken

Just like my sister Zoe
I was born broken
too

Cracking wide open
breaking

I break like a guitar string
   like a broken chord

I break like C-Sharp

I break in the elevator

I break when you flip me over
     and ask for eggs in the morning

I break beneath leather hands and big belts

I break in fast cars

I break to brass and bass and fiddles
        but never to drums

I break soft in hard places

I break quiet on rooftops and subways
        and anything that moves

I break on leopard couches, I break
        Beneath paisley quilts

I break to late sixties Dylan
        and nineties Lucinda

It takes just three days
        to break

I break into jagged pieces

Men slit their throats on me

Each time I break.

Wild Cards

Today
I read your poems
Tried to figure out
which ones were written for me
Some are easy
My initials inserted openly
Others were harder to decipher
Could have been me,
but maybe not
You say I opened my mind
but not my body,
suggesting
a greater intimacy
than I'd imagined
You stopped writing poetry
but occasionally send me
other people's work
Blowtorches of poems
you call them
Published in The Paris Review
or Atlantic Monthly
They remind us of our fathers,
missed telephone calls,
Yankee games

Wild Card made the sun rise,
I message one October morning
and you agree, drinking coffee,
waiting for a ride to the rehab center
A funny word, rehab,
when nothing can be fixed
in these broken-down houses
made of twisted bone
devoid of muscle memory
Too many cigarettes,
speedballs, and rainbow cookies
Bored silly by the gym
and its endless repetitions

Sweatpants reserved
for reading books
all Winter
and into the Spring
I wrote a few poems
Some of them might be good
but not as good as
those you send
or the ones you used to write
Slipping into Monday,
you message back,
and attach an Autumn poem
filled with breath
and shadows
We meditate
on Summertime senses
hot stoops
cold beer, reefer
while we sit
on our sinking brown couches
Twenty minutes crosstown
A thousand miles apart.

It Was A Beautiful Summer

These are my references. This is what beautiful means.

Everything was beautiful and nothing hurt – Vonnegut

You're so beautiful it hurts to look at you – Rayanne Graff, to
Angela Chase, "My So-Called Life." She was drunk, but she was
definitely correct. Sometimes it's so beautiful it hurts, different
than hot coffee and clarity and an absence of pain, different from
how you thought it could be, would ever be, one last time. The
third second wave.

*Filthy words stumbling…between the lips of your beautiful
mouth* – Lucinda Williams

Beauty every morning, lift the shades, sky hurting when it looks
at you, your river and your mean mouth, crumbling, like those
filthy words.

Every morning. It hurts to look at you, how did a New York City
summer breeze through our lives? I remember, as a kid, the
backs of my knees sticking to wicker subway seats, I remember
my railroad apartment, my room facing the F train, no air worthy
of breathing.

This summer, every morning I opened the shades, bridges
rivers, trees hurting more than the ugly, how are we deserving
as we laugh and pose and drink and lose, play music, write
poems, it still hurts, write more poems, it hurts, write poems, it
still hurts.

Danny says *It's the New Moon*, Cynthia says *Fuck the Moon*.
You're each so beautiful it hurts to look at you, why didn't
I think of that, I'm quoting an adolescent angst show
that I remember more clearly than my own life, Jordan

Castellano leaning against walls, Ricky Vasquez applying
eyeliner in the girls' room and Rayanne fucking the wrong
people, forgetting the lyrics to Ramones songs, we are never
Angela walking tightropes, bouncing higher, raising shades to
the sun, you're so beautiful it hurts, I run away as Lucinda's
words stumble through my mind, Vonnegut was right and wrong,
I write more poems, I'd rather walk the dog, there must
be a reason for this relentless beauty, every morning I raise
the shades and it's still too beautiful not to hurt a little more,
just that tiny bit more that is more than you can stand,
you close your eyes, you raise the shades, you write a song,
you write a poem, fuck the moon, beautiful summer,
you're a good left hook, beautiful summer, I give up,
raise the shades in the morning, it hurts to look.
You're so beautiful. It hurts to look away.

Fear/less: My City

You're too stupid to be afraid, my mother used to say.
Maybe I was. Wandering the streets, riding subways, entranced
by the Red Hook light hitting metal,
by the clotheslines, the pigeon coops.
Getting lost, coming home after dark, keeping secrets.

Painfully shy, my fear of people never caused fear of my city.

I was not afraid, at age seven, in Brownsville,
going to the store with my cousins,
tucking our dollar bills under our arms,
just in case.

Not afraid, at nine, walking to Coney Island
along McDonald Avenue, the rank smell
of caged chickens following us,
trying to find out if it was still all there
in the winter.

Not afraid of exploring bridges with my two silly friends from
day camp, even the ones closed to foot traffic, authorities called
to rescue us over 59th Street.

Not afraid the night I rode up to El Barrio alone because the
Young Lords had taken over a church and I was convinced that
the cause would keep me safe. And it did.

I learned the rules of the street along the way.
Who to avoid. When to keep your mouth shut. Stay away from
doorways. Walk like you know where you're going. Never take
your money out. Jump the gates. Climb the fences.
Run faster than the knife that might cut your pretty young face.
Don't tell anyone.

Survival skills. And no matter how smart, young girls do not get
away unscathed.
Some bad people, some bad nights.

But I was never afraid of my city.

A Saturday evening, in September.
We are sitting in the Garden at 6th and B, waiting to do some music.
Some poems.

My friend Ron texts me from Prague.
Explosion. Dumpster. Chelsea. Multiple injuries.
Pipe bomb explosion. Seaside Park.
Second device. 27th Street.
FBI. Homeland Security. On scene.
Cause "not yet determined."

Images flood my mind as I read.
Eagles of Death Metal. Paris.
Pulse. The gay club in Orlando.
Young people bleeding on the dance floor. Dying.
The screams.
The smell.
The Towers.
The falling bodies.

Tonight, twenty-nine injured.
Were they sleeping?
Watching television? Eating dinner?
Do we have the right to be angry?
What about our bombs?
What about the Syrian children?
What about my friends?
What have we done?

We are here, making music and poetry,
Almost as far away as Ron, in Prague,
But here. We are all here.

Greetings to everyone, messages Ron.
Be safe, my darlings.

More texts.

Are you ok? Are you ok? Are you ok?
I do the checklist.
My son's in New Jersey.
My daughter's at home down here.
Wait...Gerald lives in the Chelsea Hotel
Janis and Kevin and Jackie and Gary
and Michael and Tessa Lou and
my cousin Lynn, who hates me,
all in the neighborhood.
Are you ok? Are you ok? Are you ok?

Before 2001, we never took attendance.
Not even in the 70's when they called it
Fear City.

But we were not afraid of our city.

We were always home.
On rooftops, street corners, broken
glass, basement clubs.
There was no word for homeless.
We were always home.

I am not afraid of my city.
Neither am I intrepid.

I had my first panic attack on an Upper East Side avenue.
Armies of tight faced women marched by.
I'm afraid to ride a bike in traffic.
I have trouble catching my breath between subway stops.
My heart races when the elevator comes to a sudden halt.

But I'm no longer afraid of people.
And I am not afraid of my city.

I hate every new wrinkle and crumbling tooth but I'm glad
that I did not grow up in fear. And I got to grow old.
I remember the feeling of invulnerability.
They say all young people feel it but I don't think they do any
more. I see it in their eyes.

What in the world,
like Bowie said,
What in the world can we do?

We live.
I live.
Newscasters look at us with sad eyes.
Sometimes we get scared, too.

But when I lie in bed at night,
thirteen flights above the river,
listening to rain or traffic noise,
I am struck almost senseless
by the lights of the bridges and
the safety of my concrete walls.

I am not afraid of my city.

Escape from Gravesend

Bukowski, DiPrima, Ferlinghetti, Coltrane
Unlike my real life loves, you never let me down
In return, I've not been fickle or unfaithful
Our relationships are perfect, free of expectations and demands
You don't give me money or remember my name but you're
forever present, dead or alive, always prepared to comfort,
inspire, engage or enrage, to demand a revolution of the soul
Even if I recall nothing else when they yank the white sheet
over my head, I'll be listening to A Love Supreme, reading
a revolutionary letter, keeping Coney Island on my mind,
Bukowski's bluebird soul fluttering, because you get so alone
No matter if friends bear witness or have stories to tell,
I keep my first loves, that turquoise blue radio alongside
my bed suddenly giving a 12-year-old me the gift of Billie
singing *Willow Weep for Me* as I restlessly twist the dial,
emptiness fueling insomnia will grow into a beautiful void
someday filled with jazz and poetry books purchased
because of the Ferlinghetti cover or that Stan Getz blue,
missed those days of records and bookstores and solitary
subway rides to West 4ᵗʰ Street, adventure, illumination,
joining 2AM lost souls passing my room above the F train,
humming trains promising places to go when finally
I get the fuck out of Gravesend with its good pizza,
cages of MacDonald Avenue chickens awaiting slaughter,
a street smelling of blood, death, car wrecks, and maybe
a little bit of hope, trickling down from the elevated tracks.

Jane Ormerod's Basement*

You can't love your child because nobody loved you
You hate the Bronx because you grew up in Brooklyn
You're afraid to get a dog because they killed your cat

It's what happened in the attic
It's what happened in the basement

Years pass
Nothing matters, everything counts

Love
Loss
Life

And what else is left besides fear?

Sobriety's irrelevant if you don't want to drink
Success is compromised when everything runs smoothly
Love only happens when the garbage is taken out
Loss is another way of saying Wednesday
And life, as usual, doesn't care

There are stoops on East 10th Street
We sit in the October sun and talk about Monk and poetry,
Coney Island and the poems we wrote,
the first books we bought, HOWL and Ferlinghetti,
the people we miss, lives lost in the thick air,
indecision and a cup of coffee, club soda and a car,
we circle and return to certainty and all that matters

Love, Loss, Life and what else is left besides fear?
Could be a book title, don't ya think?

*Jane Ormerod wrote one of the best lines I've ever read:
"We refuse to enter the basement because of something that
happened in the attic," from "Belongings (Must Dress the
Character")*.

69

Unlocked

All of my stories have been told
I write new ones every morning
Yours was the last before I resigned,
cashed the blank check at Babeland
Did you see the New York moon
before the gate slammed down?
Do you still stand by your bed listening,
television humming, foot tapping,
the scent of pineapple and ginger
drifting tentatively through the window
(or was it my scent and yours mingling,
sweet rage unleashed, entangled?)
My hands lay open as I sleep,
Alone, dreamless, fucked into invisibility,
freed by indifference, my body little more
than a life support system. Again,
balanced on the borderline
We missed the high bars
The love cops locked up the playground.

There's Always a Reason

September's a new notebook
In November we eat turkey
New Year's Eve's a perfect time
for suicidal ideations
So is Valentine's Day
National Poetry Month
falls in April
Writing poems in April
is like eating Matzoh Brei
just because it's Passover
If we like Matzoh Brie
Why don't we eat some
in December
and write a poem a day
in July?
August is a dog
Daylight Savings Time
is jet lag without motion
The best Thanksgiving
is 2AM at the Remedy Diner
and the most memorable
birthday is also
the most regrettable
Easter comes in October
this year
Wear a bonnet
with your cowboy boots
Dress for Halloween
on Christmas
Close your eyes
when Death knocks
Maybe
he won't recognize you
Rebirth
in May
Count backwards
all year long
You'll never get old.

Birthdays In New York

Joe plays "She Belongs to Me"
If I could create
lyrics like that
just once
I wouldn't need
to write another word
But it's not like that

Nobody's Dylan but Dylan
Nobody's you but you
and me but me
Beatles and Lewis Carroll
weigh in
If that's what they meant
I took too much acid
at the time
to figure it out

After the party
there's another party
James Chance knocks
a few people out
with his saxophone
but by that time
I'm immobilized
Somebody put something
In my drink
as Richie said
Although his was spiked
with LSD
Or so the story goes
I was shooting too much dope
to really know

I'm sitting on the couch and
all I see
are people's legs
standing over me
I'm aware of everything but
my body won't respond
to my brain's signals
I keep repeating
I'm sick
I'm dying
Why did they do this
to me?
I'm sure that I was drugged
But maybe I drank too much
whiskey to know for sure

I can't move my legs
I can't stand up
Everyone has left
the club
I can recall standing
at the bar
with Russell, saying
hello to Lenny
and Dave Donen
I don't remember
drinking the shot
or walking to the couch

Russell, Alice and Mike
stay with me
Keep asking if I want
to go to the hospital
I refuse and finally
the bouncers walk
me out

At least she has nice boots
one of them remarks
Thanks, I respond
reflexively,
Got them at Trash
And slump over
Again

Then we're all in a cab
The driver keeps
threatening to kick
me out
Assuming that I'll
throw up
in his back seat
If only I could
Finally
We're at my door
It's taking Mike
an hour
to find the right key
*The one with the number
four,* I keep telling him
I'm getting so pissed off
I must be getting better

I sit on the couch
Russell babysits
He's an old hand
at dealing with drunks
and psychotic women
I start to recover
A few moments
of pre-contemplation
and I swear off nothing
What else did I think
might happen?
They all told me so
back in the days
of qualifications

and keychains

The following evening
I recite some poems
in the Garden
I've just learned
that my friend
Colleen Whitaker
will probably not make it
through the night.
She doesn't.
The Harvest Moon
rises again
and I ask it to be kind
To take care
of my friends
Two dear souls
A sister and brother
In my poetry world
In our world
Gone in the last
eight days
Colleen Whitaker
David Smith
Colleen Whitaker
David Smith

Repetition does not
make it real
I go home
Eat a cracker
Break a tooth
Send money
to the poets
who left the party
before they got paid

I guess we all leave
the party before
we get paid

Broke and naked
But what do I know?
I wish
I was a Rainy-Day Woman
But nobody's Dylan
but Dylan
The rest of us
keep trying
to figure it out.

On the Morning After My Birthday Again

4:30 AM,
I broil a steak
Eat in front of the tv
A Sesame Street movie
comes on
I love Sesame Street
but Elmo's voice goes right through me
I turn the sound off,
envision drunken trees
falling
on city streets
The power of memory
over existence
Blackouts allowing
indiscretions
on birthday nights
A yearly tradition,
along with angry cab drivers
who yell at me
thinking I'll throw up
in the back seat
I never do
25 years of sobriety
dented, but did not disable,
my abilities
Taxi vomit is for amateurs
The night brought
another show
My poetry
Joff's music
Danny Ray's sax
Walter's violin
Joe sang
"She Belongs to Me"
I counted out money
and drink tickets
but lost track
of the drinks

4:30 AM
I feel better than expected
Another birthday gift
besides the obvious
I don't think about the times
that I should have been dead
I don't want what I don't have
I don't throw up in cabs
We make music and art
and drink too much
Can't ask for more
when you're playing
with the house's money.

The Most Perfect Imperfect Day

It is 8:17 PM, October 27, 2015

Two years since Lou Reed died on that Sunday morning

I sit in a poetry workshop, our writing exercise inspired

by blues and Leadbelly and Memphis Minnie

But   once again

All I have left is Lou

Rarely do you remember such a perfect, imperfect day

A day of music drifting from every doorway

Skies clear, except for the teardrops of seagulls

Tai Chai in the sun at the end, telling his love, Laurie Anderson,

Lead me into the light

As a teen-ager, I was threatened with shock treatments,

Kings County incarcerations

They never followed through

Probably didn't have very good insurance

So I set my words on fire and hid my cigarettes and decades later

Joff and Danny Ray and I send Lou off

with poems

and saxophones and *Pale Blue Eyes,*

a gathering of friends

and I guess   and I wish.   and I guess   and I wish

Six words burned as quickly as my notebooks

in the pink kitchen sink

and I guess   and I wish   and I guess   and I wish

Missing from the book, but engraved in my arm

between a Coney Island Baby and

a Halloween Parade

I linger on

Rock n Roll Animal all day long

Picasso had his nasty side, too

So did Elvis, and John Lennon

But still we dance

That's All Right, Mama plays on repeat

in the Blue Room

And it's all right   and I wish   and I guess

and I wish

and all I have left is you and

what could have been one of those most perfect

imperfect days.

Acknowledgements

So many friends wandered in and out of the pages of this book. You are all my muses. From the opening poem, at Razor's Bay Area home, to the closing one, on the Lower East Side, you've breathed this book into being. No matter if you're on this planet or another one, or somewhere in the air. I'm grateful to say your names: Scott Wanneberg, David Smith, Lee McGrevin, and James "Jimmie the Saint" Tropeano. You've left your words with me and with the world.

Love and appreciation go out to everyone I've made art and music with over the last few years. Joff Wilson, Danny Ray, Walter Steding and Angello Olivieri are the core of Puma Perl and Friends, "speaking in "tongues," as Danny once put it. Also, in the mix are Joe Sztabnik, Dave Donen, Seaton (Chuckie) Hancock, Rick Eckerle, New York Junk (Joe, Cynthia Ross, Jeff Ward and Gary Barnett,) SoulCake (Joff, Sarafe, and Laura Sativa), and the Mark McKay Band, with whom I've improvised lines that grew into poems. I have the luxury problem of sharing the stage and the creative process with too many people to list individually on these pages.

Special thanks to everyone who contributed to this book. Kat Georges, Jane LeCroy, Brian Smith, and Jerry Stahl, thank you for your generosity, words, and time. Zoe Hansen, Matthew Hupert, Annie Petrie, Nicca Ray, and Maggie Rawlings Smith, thank you for your support and encouragement. Thanks to Chelle Mayer for your art in everything you do, for bringing my vision to your beautiful book cover, and, with Dennis Doyle, saving the day with the design I had created but couldn't implement, and to Ellen Berman and Dina Regine for your photography.

I have been enriched by my relationship with Beyond Baroque over the years and am grateful for their belief in me and my work, their continued support, and the opportunities they have provided. This book came about at the invitation of former Executive Director Richard Modiano. Iris Berry, my West Coast sister, stepped up as Editor and Iris of all trades, bringing the gift of her poetic insight, her knowledge of me and my work, and her production and publishing skills. As I wrote in the opening poem, which includes my first real life meeting with Iris, "I'd found my tribe." I have a great West Coast family, including my forever friend Roz Blumenstein, aka Miss Hospitality, Susan Hayden and Sharyl Holtzman, all of whom have always provided support and love.

As always, dedicated to my family: Louis, Juliet, Fran, and Diva the Wonder Dog.

About the author

Photo by Ellen Berman

Puma Perl believes in the transformative power of the arts. Diane DiPrima's work suggested to her that a Brooklyn girl could write poetry. And even leave Brooklyn. In the early 70's, she stopped by the Nuyorican Poets Café on its second night in existence, on East 6th between A and B. It was there that she learned that poetry and performance were accessible to all, regardless of class and academic achievement. And that art doesn't care what other people think you can do. Decades after the Café opened, she's still on the Lower East Side, writing, producing, performing, photographing.

Birthdays Before and After is her fifth solo collection. Her first chapbook, *Belinda and Her Friends,* was awarded the erbacce-prize for poetry in 2009 and led to her first full length collection, *knuckle tattoos,* published in 2010. *Ruby True,* an erbacce press chapbook, followed in 2012, and another full-length collection, *Retrograde* (great weather for MEDIA), was published in 2014.

Her poetry and short stories have appeared in numerous journals and anthologies including *Suitcase of Chrysanthemums* (great weather for MEDIA, 2018), *Maintenant, Red Fez, The Villager, Have a NYC, Volumes 1 and 2,* (Three Rooms Press), *Sensitive Skin,* and *City Primeval: New York, Berlin,* Prague (Editors Robert Carrithers and Louis Armand). In 2016, she received the Acker Award in the category of writing. She is also a journalist and has been awarded two honorable mentions and one first place prize by the New York Press Association for her contributions to *The Villager.*

Puma is the creator, curator, producer, and host of Puma Perl's Pandemonium, which merges two of her passions, poetry and rock and roll. As Puma Perl and Friends, she performs regularly with some of her favorite musicians who are also great friends. She has read as a solo artist and collaborated with bands throughout the United States, and in London and Prague. She's a frequent visitor to the Los Angeles area and co-hosted The Beyond Gala, a Bohemian Bacchanal Celebrating 50 Years of Beyond Baroque.

She continues to be transformed.

About the cover artist

Chelle Mayer, drawing pictures before she could talk, is a full-time artist from New England who travels with her dog Bessie in a big yellow graffiti-ed van. Born to a cartoon, she draws inspiration from music, poetry, adventures, collaborations and comic books, resulting in brightly colored creations. You can view her art posted under peaceful shades across the web. Instagram.com/peacefulshades

Other Beyond Baroque Books

Every Bird Helps: A Cancer Journal
By Phoebe Macadams $10.00

Block Island Latitudes/Manhattan Island Suite
By Michael C Ford $10.00

Pacific Coast Poetry Series
Wide Awake Edited
By Suzanne Lummis $18.00

Our Foreigner
By Nance Van Winkel $18.00

In Order of Disappearance
By Carine Topal $18.00

Made in the USA
Coppell, TX
02 March 2020

16365921R00060